101 Coolest Thir in Tokyo

© 2016 101 Coolest Things

All rights reserved. No part of this publication may be reproduced, distributed, or transmitted in any form or by any means, including photocopying, recording, or other electronic or mechanical methods, without the prior written permission of the publisher, except in the case of brief quotations embodied in critical reviews and certain other noncommercial uses permitted by copyright law.

Introduction

So you're going to Tokyo, huh? You lucky lucky thing! You are sure in for a treat because Tokyo is truly one of the most magical cities on this planet.

Around the city, you can find some of the most incredible galleries and museums in Asia, there is an abundance of food that will satisfy even the pickiest of palettes, there are wonderful experiences to be had like traditional tea ceremonies, there are endless bars and clubs, and there are even beautiful parks dotted around the city

In this guide, we'll be giving you the low down on:
- the very best things to shove in your pie hole, from street food dessert stands to Michelin star restaurants
- the best shopping so that you can take a little piece of Japan back home with you, whether that's in the form of an authentic robe or a piece of fine Japanese china
- incredible festivals, whether you're into traditional Japanese dancing or you want to check out a religious festival at a temple
- the coolest historical and cultural sights that you simply cannot afford to miss from ancient Shinto shrines to incredible art galleries

- the best places to have a few cups of sake and to party like a local

- and tonnes more coolness besides!

Let's not waste any more time – here are the 101 coolest things not to miss in Tokyo!

1. Have an Arty Day in Japan's Largest Gallery

Tokyo National Museum is the largest art gallery in the country, and one of the largest in the world. Once inside, you'll be able to discover more than 110,000 objects of art and archaeology from around Asia, including important pieces such as the one of the first representations of Buddha from 1st century Pakistan, and Jomon pottery from 10,000 BC. Culture vultures will be bowled away.

2. Eat a Sushi Breakfast at Tsukiji Market

When you talk about Tokyo markets, there is one market that needs to be explored above all the others. Against the odds, it's a fish market, but trust us when we say it's more than a bit special. This is, in fact, the largest and busiest fish market in the whole world. While you probably aren't in town to pick up a bucket of wholesale fish, you should absolutely indulge in one of the stalls that sells breakfast sushi. You can bet your bottom dollar that it will be the freshest sushi of your life.

3. Explore Japanese Tradition at the National Noh Theatre

Japan is a country full of ancient traditions, and Noh theatre is a classical type of Japanese performance that dates right back to the 14th century. With this kind of theatre, the movement is very slow, the costumes are elaborate and very heavy, the language is poetic, and the stories are based on ancient legends. If you want to check out a performance for yourself, you can watch a show at the National Noh Theatre in Tokyo.

4. Take in a Sumo Wrestling Match

Sumo wrestling is officially the national sport of Japan, and if you are the sporting type, you'll want to take in a live match on your Japan travels. In Tokyo, the official Sumo tournaments take place in January, May, and September, so this is the time to look out for tickets. The place to watch is the Kokugikan stadium, and do spend the extra on ringside seats if you can. Sumo wrestling tournaments are an all-day affair, so it definitely pays to be comfortable and to have a good view.

5. Indulge Your Inner Carnivore at a Japanese BBQ

There is more to Japanese cuisine than sushi and sashimi, and if you are more of a carnivore than a fish lover, you need to become well acquainted with the art of Japanese barbecue sooner rather than later. Japanese barbecue is known as Yakiniku on the streets, and it's big news in Japan's capital city. Nakara is one of the best barbecue restaurants in Tokyo, with high quality meat and some interesting cuts. The wagyu beef is truly unbelievable, and their beef tongue is a firm favourite with locals.

6. Search Out Ceramics at Mashiko Pottery Fair

Japan has a long history of outstandingly beautiful handicrafts, and its pottery culture is second to none. If you really want to get to grips with stunning pottery in Japan, waste no time and head straight to Mashiko, a town not far from Tokyo. As soon as you arrive and see the photographs of potters at work in the train station, you will understand the town's dedication to all things made from clay. And to buy some exceptional pieces yourself, be sure to visit the twice yearly Mashiko Pottery Fair, which sets up in April and November.

7. Understand Japanese Animation at Ghibli Museum

Mitaka is a city located in the Western part of the Tokyo metropolis, and though it's not ordinarily visited by tourists, there is one good reason to visit - the Ghibli Museum. This is the museum of the Japanese animation studio, Ghibli, whose work includes the critical and commercial success, Spirited Away. You'll find rooms filled with original sketchbooks, 3D figures based on the studio's characters, interactive filmography exhibitions, and screenings of their rare works.

8. Sample a Green Tea Beer

In a very short space of time in Tokyo, you'll become aware that the Japanese people are crazy for matcha tea. You can find matcha lattes, matcha cakes, and many other types of matcha goodness. Perhaps the strangest that we have encountered is matcha beer. Well, that's exactly what you can try at the Matcha Beer Garden. The taste is certainly unique and refreshing, but it takes a few sips to get used to it. Matcha croquettes are also sold if you fancy a nibble!

9. Have Your Laptop Blessed at Kanda Shrine

If you're into shrines, you're in the right country. Japan has an endless amount of them! But one of the strangest and most special of them all is Kanda Shrine, which is where the ancient Japanese culture meets the 21st century with a bang. When visiting this shrine in Tokyo, be sure to bring your smartphone, your tablet device, and your laptop with you. The Shinto religion holds that absolutely every object has a spiritual essence, and the Shinto priests here will be happy to bless your electronics!

10. Take a Stroll Around Little Edo

Just outside of Tokyo, there is a fascinating small town that goes by the name of Kawagoe, and it is otherwise affectionately titled Little Edo because there is a great deal in the town that looks just as it would have in the Edo period of history, which extends from the early 17th century to the mid 19th century. The main street of Kurazukuri street is the place to go to see many traditional Kurazukuri style houses, many of which have been transformed into shops where you can purchase traditional crafts.

11. Ease Your Muscles in the Hot Springs of Hakone

On your trip in Japan, you're likely to hear the word "onsen" more than a few times. So what does it mean? An onsen is essentially the word for a hot spring, or the word for a resort built around a hot spring. And the centre of onsens in Japan is Hakone. There are tonnes and tonnes of natural hot springs in Hakone, and because it's a stone's throw from Tokyo, it's a popular escape for big city types. We recommend the Sounkaku onsen, which is nestled between mountain peaks.

12. Drink at a Dinosaur Themed Beer Bar!

You love beer – of course you do! You love dinosaurs – err, of course you do? Well, in Tokyo you have the rare opportunity to combine the best of these two worlds in a dinosaur themed beer bar called Beer Saurus (of course that's what it's called!). This is more than just a novelty bar, there are actually more than 100 types of beer served up inside, from right across the world. And in a pricey city like Tokyo, the 6-8pm happy hour for half price beers cannot be beaten.

13. Slurp on Ramen Day and Night

Ramen noodles are a famous Japanese dish right over the world, but actually, the first time they appeared on a menu in Japan was only in 1910, and it was actually Chinese cooks in Japan that created the dish. Versions of these soba noodles, wet and dry, spicy and served with handfuls of herbs, are now a staple of Japanese cuisine, and you'll find heaping bowls of ramen with broth, seafood, meat, veggies, and egg all over Tokyo.

14. View Tokyo From the Tallest Building in Japan

The Tokyo skyline is staggeringly impressive, with a huge number of towering buildings, but the most impressive of them all is the Tokyo Skytree. Standing at 634 metres in height, this is easily the tallest building in Japan, and it's the second tallest structure on the planet. What's more, you can scale the building and get a killer view from one of its two observation decks, the tallest of which is at 450 metres. That's a truly dizzying height so this isn't one for people who suffer from vertigo.

15. Get a Comfort Food Fix With Karaage

Japanese grub isn't exactly well known for being full of comfort food options, but search and you shall find. The comfort food at the end of the rainbow in Japan is karaage, otherwise known as Japanese fried chicken. What sets apart karaage from other varieties of fried chicken around the world is that the batter is extraordinarily crispy. That's because potato starch is used instead of the standard breadcrumbs. It really makes the difference, and if you're a fried chicken fan, you'll undoubtedly be converted to the Japanese style.

16. Get Artsy at the Mori Art Museum

While most people don't visit Japan specifically to go to galleries, if you have an interest in the arts, an afternoon in the Mori Art Museum is certainly an afternoon well spent. There are no permanent collections here, and the collections on display are always varied but contemporary. One month you might see something from Japanese comic artists and the next from textile artists from the Middle East. The museum is also located on the 53rd and 54th floors of a building, so it offers great views of Tokyo.

17. Spend the Night in a Capsule Hotel

Space is the most valuable commodity in Tokyo, and you'll find this out when you try and book a hotel room. If you want a suite, you will pay for it. To save your money, staying at a capsule hotel is a penny pincher that could work for you. It is exactly what is says on the tin – a capsule with a bed, and, well, nothing else. If you are at all claustrophobic, this probably won't suit you, but if not, why not give it a whirl?

18. Watch a Traditional Kabuki Drama

Kabuki is a traditional form of theatre in Japan that dates all the way back to the Edo period, and a trip to Tokyo wouldn't be complete without taking in a Kabuki show. This type of performance is characterised by the exaggerated movements of the actors, the crazy wigs, outlandish make-up, and incredibly elaborate costumes. The best place to catch a Kabuki performance in Tokyo is at the Kabukiza Theatre where you will even be provided with English headsets so you can follow all the action.

19. Have a Cup of Coffee With Moomin

Japan is a country that is absolutely rammed full of cuteness, and there are many cute cafés based on cartoon characters and animation strewn around Tokyo. Perhaps the cutest of them all is the Moomin Bakery and Café, unsurprisingly centred around the Moomin cartoon character. The bread here is really good, and the rye bread is exceptional. But what makes this place extra cute, is that if you are dining alone, the staff will sit a Moomin at your table with you for company.

20. Understand Japanese Handicrafts at Japanese Folk Crafts Museum

Japan has a dynamic arts culture, but it's important not to forget the arts and crafts traditions of ordinary Japanese people, and that's exactly what this museum in Tokyo is dedicated to. The museum was created in a 1930 as a way to showcase the beautiful objects that Japanese people use in their everyday lives, with a collection of more than 17,000 hand crafted objects, including ceramics, woodwork, and textiles.

21. Take a Nap in a Love Hotel

Perhaps you have already heard of Japan's famous (or should that be infamous?) love hotels. These are hotels with rooms that can be rented by the hour, mainly for a bit of rumpy pumpy. But actually, many love hotels are not as seedy as they sound. Hotel Famy in Tokyo, for example, has karaoke rooms, video games, and spaces to work. Whether you want to have some fun or simply take a nap, a love hotel could be a surprisingly great place to recharge your batteries.

22. Drink 70 Beers on Tap at Popeye

While sake is probably the best known drink in Japan, the local people certainly do like to down a glass of beer or two as well. The really nice thing about Popeye bar in Tokyo, is that you aren't just served up bottles of beer from a refrigerator. They actually have seventy types of beer on tap, and the knowledgeable staff are really passionate about the bar's beer choices. And if you want to sample something local, there are plenty of Japanese microbrews on offer.

23. Throw Beans for Setsubun

If you want to experience some of traditional Japan on your trip to Tokyo, it's a great idea to coincide trip with the traditional festivals. Setsubun is a festival that takes place on the last day before spring in the beginning of February. It's customary to chase away evil spirits during this festival, and one way of doing so is by throwing roasted coffee beans around the house. In Tokyo, a whole bean throwing festival takes place at the Zojoji temple.

24. Eat Dinner Served by Ninjas

Tokyo has its fair share of strange restaurants, and one of the strangest is Ninja Akasaka. Yup, staff dressed as ninjas will take your order and serve you your food for the evening. You will also be immersed in a world of a Japanese castle, with incredible decorative details, and even a magician to entertain you at your table. There's never any shortage of surprises when you eat dinner at Ninja Akasaka, and guess what? The food is awesome too.

25. Play Beach Volleyball in the Centre of Tokyo

The Tokyo Metro area isn't so well known for having spectacular beaches, but if you do want to enjoy a little beach time, you're in luck, because there is an artificial beach called Odaiba, which is a constructed island in Tokyo Bay. There are volleyball nets constructed along the beach, so if you are looking to escape the high rises and want to enjoy a fun, outdoor activity, a game of volleyball on the beach with friends you've made in the hostel could be just the ticket.

26. Learn How to Roll Your Own Sushi

While you are in Japan, there is absolutely no doubt that you will be chowing down on plenty of sushi for breakfast, lunch, and dinner. But wouldn't it be impressive if you could actually learn how to make sushi for authentic Japanese dinner parties back at home? The Tokyo Sushi Academy is absolutely the place to pick up this skill. Classes are both educational and fun, and you'll learn how to make different types of sushi such as California rolls and Nigiri.

27. Visit the Famed Meiji Shrine

There is no shortage of Shinto shrines to be found around Tokyo, but perhaps the most famous of them all is the Meiji shrine. Created in 1920, this shrine is dedicated to the deified spirits of Emperor Meiji and his wife. This shrine is great to visit when you want a peaceful morning escape from the usual hectic nature of the city as the shrine is situated within seventy hectares of beautiful forest. Inside, you can also find a treasure museum that contains many beautiful items once owned by the Emperor and Empress.

28. Slurp Down Udon Noodles Every Day

If your noodle experience is limited to packets of dried noodles submerged in hot water, you are in for a treat on your trip to Tokyo. Udon noodles are much thicker than the packet noodles you are used to, they are made from wheat, and they have a deliciously chewy texture. They can be served up in piping hot bowls of broth, and you might also find them served cold with a dipping sauce, which means that udon noodles are the perfect dish for summer and winter weather!

29. Take Tea at Rikugien Garden

If you are looking for some peaceful respite from the bustle of Tokyo City, Rikugien is a park hidden away in the centre of the city. There are lawn areas, a flower garden, and a forest, but the highlight is the teahouse where you can experience an authentic Japanese tea ceremony, and take the time to replenish your body and mind with a few moments of peace and a steaming cup of green tea.

30. Explore Folk Japan at Nihon Minka-en

Tokyo to Kawasaki is just 14 minutes away by train, and this small city on the fringe of the capital is well worth a visit, if only to visit the incredible Nihon Minka-En open air museum. This museum is dedicated to preserving traditional Japanese folk houses, which you can walk around and explore in the open air. Inside you will find a water mill, a storehouse on stilts, and even a traditional craft hall that sometimes has indigo dying workshops. Tours in English are available too.

31. Learn About the Japanese Silk Trade

Yokohama is the second largest city in Japan by population, but less frequented by tourists. It's worth making the trip to the city, just half an hour outside of Tokyo, for the Yokohama Silk Museum alone. There is a beautiful display of Japanese silk clothing from many periods of Japanese history, and you can also learn about the process of turning the silkworm threads into actual garments. Another highlight is the museum shop where you can purchase stunning silk scarves to take home with you, and there are even food products made with silk that are sold there too!

32. Buy Outlandish Clothes in Harajuku Boutiques

Japan is a country full of contradictions. While it's a place full of ancient traditions and temples that are hundreds of years old, there is also a vibrant counterculture that the youth of Tokyo is spearheading. Walk around the Harajuku neighbourhood and you'll see teenagers dressed up in all kinds of crazy garb. If you want to emulate them and embrace your inner teen, this is absolutely the place to do your shopping. You'll be a Hello Kitty cosplayer yet!

33. Catch your Own Dinner at Zaou Fishing Boat Café

There is no shortage of wacky dining experiences to be found in the Japanese capital city, and one that's up there has to be the Zaou Fishing Boat Café in the Shinjuku area. In this restaurant, you are invited to catch your own dinner. You'll be given a fishing rod and some bait, and the rest is up to you. Fortunately, this place isn't all novelty. Once you have caught your fish, they will grill it to perfection.

34. Celebrate LGBT Pride in Tokyo

Life is not especially easy for the LGBT population of Japan. With no legal recognition of same sex relationships and a conservative culture, gay people across the country are still fighting to be given equal rights. You can join in with the fight at the annual LGBT Pride event in Tokyo, which takes place in May each year. During this festival there is a big party in Yoyogi Park and a parade that makes its way through the Harajuku neighbourhood. Wave that rainbow flag with pride!

35. Chow Down on Raw Pig Testicles in Tokyo

Okay, this probably doesn't sound like the most appealing thing on your Japan "to-do" list, and quite honestly, it might only appeal to hardcore adventurers, but if that sounds like you, then the raw pig testicles are just waiting to be eaten. The place to go for this infamous dish is "piss alley" in Tokyo where you'll find bars and food stalls right on the street. This dish is also served with a raw egg – double the raw for double the fun.

36. Get Commercial at the Museum of Advertising and Marketing

When you imagine Tokyo in your head, you probably imagine bright lights and illuminated billboards covering the wide city streets. And indeed, this is a common sight in Tokyo, and what better way to get under the skin of Tokyo's commercial culture than at the Museum of Advertising and Marketing? Their permanent collection shows how advertising in Japan has changed from the Edo period up to the present day, and there are always different temporary exhibits as well.

37. Have the Authentic Karaoke Box Experience

A trip to Japan is not a trip to Japan without some ritual humiliation in the form of a late night karaoke session. Tokyo might just be the karaoke capital of the world. Karaoke boxes (private karaoke rooms) can be found in streets close to train stations all over the Japanese capital. Yes, there will be a lot of songs in Japanese, but most will have English classics, so make sure that you brush up on your favourite Elvis and ABBA tracks.

38. Relax With a Cold Beer and Skewers of Yakitori

When you need to have a break from eating sushi for breakfast, lunch, and dinner, it's time to switch to some skewers of yakitori. Yakitori is essentially skewers of meat, typically chicken, and they date all the way back to the 17th century in Japan. These days, there are thousands of places where you can enjoy yakitori in Tokyo but we recommend Iseya. This is a down and dirty yakitori shop that's 80 years old with absolutely no frills. But the flavour is out of this world, and it tastes even better when washed down with a cold beer.

39. Buy Traditional Japanese Robes at the Oriental Bazaar

If you're reaching the end of your Japanese adventure and you still have some shopping to do, head straight to Oriental Bazaar in Tokyo, which is probably the best known souvenir shop in the country. You can find all kinds of objects like Japanese pottery and books about the country, but something really special here is the selection of authentic Japanese robes. The prices here are better than you will find anywhere else in the city, and taking home a robe is a beautiful reminder of a beautiful country.

40. Embrace Your Inner Child at the Tokyo Kite Museum

This is certainly not one of the major museums to be found in Tokyo. In fact, it's located in a room above a restaurant. But if you have a fondness for Japanese crafts and the days you spent flying kites as a kid, this charming Tokyo attraction will be right up your street. The space contains around 300 kites, many of which are hand painted with the most incredible detail, depicting stories from Japanese folk tales and legends.

41. Attend the Magical Toro Nagashi

Toro Nagashi is one of the most incredible celebrations in all of Japan. If you make it to the country in August, you will get to experience this magical festival. Toro Nagashi is essentially the practice of floating paper lanterns on water, which represents souls departing in a beautiful way to the next realm. The very best place for this is in Sumida Park where you can watch the lanterns floating along the river.

42. Try Japanese Whiskey at Zoetrope

If you want to try the local spirits on a trip to Tokyo, be sure to head Zoetrope in the Nishi-Shinjuka area, a bar that specialises in Japanese whiskies. The bar has a very impressive collection of 300 whiskies, more than any other in Tokyo, and some of the whiskies aren't even being made any more. If you have no idea what to order, let the knowledgeable staff take you on a journey through Japanese whiskey that you will never forget.

43. Rent a Tandem Bike in Yoyogi Park

Although Tokyo is a large and bustling city, it also has a good number of green spaces where you can walk around, find some peace, and get back to nature. Yoyogi Park is one of the largest parks in the city. If you happen to be travelling with a partner, one of the most romantic things to do is rent a tandem bicycle in the park, and cycle your way through the greenery together.

44. Brush up Your Japanese Language Skills

We are not even gonna front – Japanese is a very difficult language to get a handle on. If, however, you are staying in the country for a longer period of time, it can be really rewarding to learn some of the language so that you can actually exchange pleasantries with the local people. There are Japanese language schools all over the city, but the Genki Japanese Language & Culture School is a great option because they run a Japanese language survival course, specifically designed for tourists with no prior knowledge of the language.

45. Indulge a Sweet Tooth in Candy Store Alley

Do you have something of a sweet tooth? If so, you might want to skip another temple viewing session, and find your way to Candy Store Alley in Tokyo instead. This is officially known as Ameyoko, and as you might expect, you can find all kinds of delicious sweet treats here. In the 20th century, this also become a "black market" market, so this tucked away alley has more of an interesting past than you might expect.

46. Find Something Special at the Antique Jamboree

If you are the kind of person who loves to hunt out special objects, the annual Antique Jamboree in Tokyo will be right up your alley. Hosted every August, this is the largest antiques fair in the whole country, and many would say the best. More than 500 antiques vendors are invited to showcase their special items, and you can get your hands on objects such as vintage kimonos, manga art, precious metal items, beautiful Japanese pottery, and much more besides. Beats a tacky souvenir shop any day!

47. Get the Authentic Japan Experience With Couchsurfing

It is no secret that Japan isn't exactly the cheapest country in the world to travel. If you are travelling on a tight budget, you can save money on accommodation by signing up for Couchsurfing.com. With this website, you can find local Japanese people who have a spare bed or a spare couch, and they offer their space for free. As well as being a great saving money tool, Couchsurfing offers the opportunity for genuine cultural exchange. You will actually get to experience how local people live instead of staring at the hotel walls.

48. Go Back to School With a Japanese School Lunch

You, like most people, probably have regular nightmare flashbacks of gloopy school dinners. But you might just gain an appreciation for those good ol' days on a trip to Tokyo, which happens to house a café that serves up school dinner fare, Kyushokutoban. All of the meals come out on uniform stainless steel trays alongside bottles of milk, and actually, the food is pretty good. You can chow down on bowls of noodle soup and indulge in Japanese chicken curry. Yummy.

49. Go Vintage Shopping at Haight & Ashbury

Tokyo is, without a doubt, a shopping lover's paradise. But when you visit a city for the first time, it can be really hard to know about the places to pick up something extra special. Well, if you are something of a fashionista and you prefer to pick up your clothes in quirky vintage shops, we can totally recommend a trip to Haight & Ashbury in the trendy

Shimokitazawa neighbourhood. This isn't the kind of vintage store where you have to rummage through bins of clothing. Everything is very carefully selected, and new items are added every day.

50. Visit the Residence of the Emperor of Japan

Any building that houses an emperor is bound to be something extra special, and the Tokyo Imperial Palace does not disappoint. The palace and its surrounds are, in fact, so grand, that they were valued more highly than all Californian real estate combined during the 1980s Japan property bubble. Tour the palace and gardens and you'll soon understand why. Opulence doesn't even begin to describe it, with banquet halls, music halls, and perfectly manicured lawns.

51. Spend the Night in a Traditional Ryokan

A ryokan is essentially a traditional Japanese Inn, and if you are looking for a more traditional accommodation option, this is ideal. The buildings are often very beautiful, and the experience authentically Japanese – by which we mean that you might have to figure out your bill without speaking English! Meals are often included too, and these will include lavish set menu dinners of up to 15 courses. If you're looking to treat yourself, get into it.

52. Indulge a Train Geek at The Railway Museum

Are you something of a train nerd? First of all, you will have a whale of a time riding on the high speed trains around the country, but secondly, it's absolutely imperative that you visit Tokyo's Railway Museum to indulge your inner train geek. Inside, you will find 30 railway cars, railway model dioramas, and more. But the highlight has to be the chance to drive a steam locomotive in a high-tech simulation.

53. Visit the Temple of the Goddess of Mercy

Tokyo is often thought of as a city right on the cutting edge of contemporary culture, but there are also many historic sights and attractions in the city, and the Senso-ji temple is one of them. In fact, this ancient Buddhist temple was created in the year 628, making it the oldest temple in all of Tokyo, and one of the most important historic sites in Japan. This temple is also where Tokyo's largest festival, Sanja Matsuri, takes place, taking over the temple area for 3-4 days in the late spring each year.

54. Be Wowed by the Brass Buddha, Daibutsu

Since the small city of Kamakura is just an hour away from Tokyo by train, it is the perfect place for a fun day trip. The stand out attraction in Kamakura has to be a giant brass Buddha that dates back to the mid 13th century, and you can still spot some of the ancient gold gilding on the Buddha's ears. This daibutsu (that's the word from a giant Buddha icon) is the second largest in all of Japan, and since it is hollow, you can also enjoy the unique experience of venturing inside the Buddha.

55. Have a Day of Learning at the Edo-Tokyo Museum

The Edo period of Japan between 1603 and 1868 is when the country was ruled under the Tokugawa shogunate. In this period, rule was strict, but the country flourished economically. If you want to learn more about this period of the country's history, be sure to pay a visit to the impressive Edo-Tokyo Museum. The museum specifically focuses on the city in this period, and you can find scale models of towns and buildings from the Edo period inside.

56. Wander Around the Hama Rikyu Garden

Although Tokyo can certainly be a frantic place, there's also no shortage of green spaces where you can relax and feel the weight of the world slide from your shoulders. Hama Rikyu Garden is a beautiful space that was originally built to act as a feudal lord's garden and duck hunting residence in the Edo period, and vestiges of this can still be seen around the gardens. We are particularly enamoured by the seawater ponds that change their levels with the tides.

57. Get Scientific at Miraikan

Tokyo and Japan in general are known as places of history and culture, but if your leanings are more towards the scientific side of things, don't fear because you can have a great day out at Mirakain, the National Museum of Emerging Science and Innovation. Our favourite thing in the museum is the display of real time data from seismometers located around the country. They show how the country is vibrating all of the time.

 ## 58. Say Hi to Honey Bees in Tokyo

You might not think that Tokyo is the best place to get back to nature, and for the most part you would be right, but the Ginko Honey Bee Farm is a place where city life and nature meet. The rooftop bee farm opened in 2006, and since then has been committed to producing honey in the urban setting of Tokyo. At the moment, they are producing something like 300 kilograms of honey per year. Why not head to the rooftop and check out the operation for yourself?

59. Indulge in a Japanese Breakfast at the Girandole

At a cost per night of $700, there aren't that many people who can afford to stay at the Park Hyatt when they visit Tokyo. But you don't have to spend so much money to taste some of the hotel's luxury, because you can enjoy a decadent Japanese breakfast at the hotel's restaurant for a much more respectable $40. The breakfast contains a pot of steamed rice, some soft tofu, salmon grilled with a crispy skin, and lots of tea.

60. Pass a Free Morning at the Japanese Paper Museum

Okay, so you probably aren't journeying all the way to Japan to learn about its paper, but if you are stuck for something to do on a drizzly Tokyo morning, a trip to the Japanese Paper Museum can be unexpectedly fun and educational. In the museum, you can learn about the history of manufacturing paper in Japan and around the world. You can also take part in paper making workshops, which kids are sure to enjoy.

61. Enjoy a Night of Cocktails at Gen Yamamoto

After a long day of sightseeing, the first thing you want to do is to sip on a decadent cocktail in a comfortable atmosphere. For this, there is no better place than Gen Yamamoto. The thing we really like about this bar is that the cocktails are smaller than normal, and this means that you can drink more of them! We also love the local ingredients that are used in the cocktails, such as Japanese arrowroot and tart winter cherries.

62. Shop for Folk Crafts at Takumi

If you only have a couple of days left in Tokyo and you still need to go souvenir shopping, one of the best places to pick up something really special is at Takumi, a shop in the Ginza district of the city that specialises in traditional Japanese crafts. You can find items such as ceramics, folk toys, textiles, and more. We particularly like that every object has a written description in the store so you can feel a far greater connection to the souvenirs you choose to buy.

63. Chow Down on Gyoza at Harajuku Gyoza Lou

While you might think that gyoza are ten a penny in Japan, they actually aren't such a popular or known food in Tokyo, and you might have to seek them out. If you do so, the place to sample the very best gyoza of your life is at Harajuku Gyoza Lou. Now, you shouldn't expect anything fancy because this is a no frills joint with just two types of gyoza – fried or steamed. But they are cheap and absolutely delicious.

64. Pray for Good Grades at the Yushima Seido Temple

Most of the temples that you will find around Tokyo are Buddhist temples, but Yushima Seido is an exception, and one of the only Confucian temples to be found. Confucianism stresses the practice of having to improve yourself through endeavour, and study, and because of this, it's a very popular place in the city for students who want to improve their grades. The temple dates back to the 17th century, and it's a fantastic example of how Chinese culture has influenced Japan.

65. Dance at Rinko Park's Bon Festival

As you travel around Japan, you might hear the words Bon or Bon Odori on the streets. The idea of these festivities is that you essentially honour the spirit of your ancestors, and during this time in Tokyo, there are often many fun outdoor parties. One of our favourites is at Rinko Park, where each year you can find incredible taiko drumming performances, chow down on Japanese curry in the street, and drink beers in the open air – perfect!

66. Sink an Outdoor Pint at the Lumine Beer Garden

If you are visiting Tokyo in the warm summer months, there is little more appealing than sinking a beer or two in the Tokyo sunshine. Fortunately, Tokyo has a growing beer garden culture, and one of the loveliest beer gardens of them all is the Lumine Beer Garden in the trendy Shinjuku neighbourhood. The all you can eat barbecue grub makes the beer go down even better.

67. Beautify Your Skin With Snails

If you are the kind of person who loves to visit spas and saunas when you take a vacation, you are in luck because Tokyo is home to so many of them. But if you want to try something a little different to another body scrub or soak in the Jacuzzi, you can definitely change things up a bit at the Ci:z Labo spa and salon. They have a very unique treatment called the snail facial. A variety of massages and masks are used in tandem with snail mucus to ensure that it penetrates the skin.

68. Indulge an Inner Carnivore at Katayama

Japanese food can be very fish heavy, but if you are a meat lover through and through, you won't have to worry because Tokyo also caters very well to meat eaters, particularly if you find your way to Katayama, a restaurant that serves up very meat plates with meat sourced from both Japan and Australia. The highlight of the menu has to be dabincho, which is rump steak with the sinew carefully cut off.

69. Eat Rice Dumplings From Kototoi Dango

While Japan might not be as well known for its desserts and candies as its savoury dishes, those with a sweet tooth won't be disappointed on a trip to Kototoi Dango. This small teahouse specialises in rice dumplings flavoured with different types of bean paste: red, white, or miso. It is more common for people to buy a box of six and take them home, but there is also an on-site café so you can enjoy a green tea and a rice dumpling in a serene atmosphere.

70. Spend a Rainy Afternoon at the Japanese Sword Museum

If you find yourself in Tokyo on a rainy day and you can't face walking around temples and shopping streets, fear not because the city is also home to plenty of museums and indoor attractions. One of our favourite rainy day places is the Japanese Sword Museum. This place is slightly off the beaten track in a residential neighbourhood, but that means you won't be jostling arm to arm with other tourists. There are dozens of swords on display.

71. Discover Japanese Ceramics at Musee Tomo

Pottery and porcelain work are some of Japan's oldest art forms, but if you want to explore a more contemporary side of Japanese ceramics, you can't do much better than a visit to Musee Tomo. The museum is named after one of the country's leading ceramicists, Kikuchi Tomo, and you can see some of his work on display inside the museum, as well as works by other contemporary ceramics practitioners, and the temporary exhibits are switched every few months.

72. Try the Typical Onigiri Snack From a 7-11

While it's true that Tokyo is an awesome city for food, you might not always have the time, money, or inclination to enjoy a sit down meal in a fancy restaurant. Sometimes you just need something quick that you can eat while on the go, and in this situation, you need to become acquainted with the multitude of 7/11 shops around Tokyo. Onigiri are rice balls wrapped in seaweed with some kind of filling inside. Some popular fillings include miso flavour, salmon roe, and even Japanese plum.

73. Take in a Show at the Tokyo Metropolitan Theatre

While you are in Tokyo, you will no doubt want to do some fun things with your evenings besides eating in restaurants and going to bars, and something to get all dressed up for is a night at the Tokyo Metropolitan Theatre. The concert hall and theatre is a fairly recent addition to Tokyo, and has wonderful acoustics that make it especially brilliant for music shows. Do keep up to date with the theatre's programme, because you could have the opportunity to witness the Tokyo Metropolitan Symphony Orchestra.

 74. Visit 19th Century Candy Shops

If you have something of a sweet tooth but you'd prefer to avoid the mass produced candies that you can find in every 7/11 across Tokyo, it can be a very good idea to visit Little Edo, which is a small town just outside of Tokyo that has kept much of its traditional architecture. Something really special in Little Edo is the abundance of traditional sweet shops. Our favourite of the whole lot might be Tamariki Seika, where you can also see how the candies are made.

75. Skate Outside at Tokyo Midtown Ice Rink

If you can brave the cold, it can be really wonderful to visit Tokyo in the winter months where the whole place illuminates and becomes filled with festive charm. One of our favourite winter activities in Tokyo is skating at the outdoor Midtown Ice Rink. Because this is an outdoor rink, it is only constructed in the coldest months of the year. As you skate around, you will be wowed by all of the tall buildings surrounding you in the midtown area.

76. Take a Walking Tour Around the Imperial Palace East Garden

The Tokyo Imperial Palace, the palace of the Emperor of Japan, is a very enjoyable building, but the Imperial Palace East Garden outside of the building might be the most enjoyable part of a trip there. Although the greenery and tranquillity of the garden is great, the thing we like the most about the garden is to get right up close to the huge stones that are used to build the castle. Free guided walking tours of the garden are available every Saturday at 1pm.

77. Enjoy All Night Fish & Chips at Malins

Okay, so when you visit Tokyo, indulging in a fish and chips supper probably isn't the first thing on your to do list. But if you are partial to a warming plate of fish and chips, we can wholeheartedly recommend Malins in the Roppongi district of the city. Malins is a relatively recent addition to Tokyo's culinary scene, but it's already left a very favourable impression thanks to its crisp golden batter and its soft flakes of fish. Even better, this restaurant is open right throughout the night until 9am!

78. Shop Organic at the Earth Day Market

As Tokyo is a big city, there are concerns about the way that the city can become more sustainable, and one of the ways that you can see Green Tokyo in action is by visiting the Earth Day Market, which takes place in Yoyogi Park every April. The market is held over the course of a weekend, and only producers and sellers who are committed to environmental sustainability and organic produce are allowed to sell their wares. You'll find everything from organic fruit and veg to handmade folk crafts inside.

79. Take Part in a Tea Ceremony at Hama Rikyu Gardens

We have already mentioned how much we love the Hama Rikyu gardens in Tokyo, but beyond the picturesque scenery, it's also a place where you can experience a traditional Japanese tea ceremony at a relatively low cost. Unlike many other tea houses in Tokyo, at this place you can simply show up without a reservation, and the location couldn't be more picturesque, located on the banks of a seawater pond. The cost of the tea ceremony is an affordable 510 yen.

80. Take in a Movie at the National Film Centre

While all the sights and attraction in Tokyo are incredible, there are times when you can't quite face another museum, and all you want to do is watch a great movie, right? When that moment strikes, there is no better place to relax and watch a film than at the National Film Centre. This is the only place in the country that is totally dedicated to the study and preservation of cinema. Almost all of the movies here are Japanese, and not all have English subtitles so be sure to enquire before buying the popcorn.

81. Indulge in Japanese Comfort Food: Katsu Curry

When you think of countries in the world where you might want to enjoy a piping hot curry, India or Thailand might be top of your list. While Japan might not be as appreciated in the curry stakes, there is still some delicious curry to be had. You might think that Indian Buddhists brought curry to Japan, but actually, it's a much more recent Japanese dish, and it was brought to Japan by the British following the Second World War. Katsu Curry typically includes succulent breaded chicken and root vegetables in a rich curry sauce. The best place to stop for a heaping bowl of the stuff is Imakatsu in Tokyo.

82. Try Urban Fishing at Ichigaya Fishing Centre

If your idea of the perfect vacation is to spend hours and hours fishing, you might not think that Tokyo is the ideal holiday destination for you, but you could be in for a surprise. The Ichigaya Fishing Centre offers fishing in the heart of the city for all urban anglers. The fish of choice in the ponds of the centre is carp, and if you reach a certain weight with your catch in one hour, you will receive another hour for free!

83. Learn About Sumo at the Sumo Museum

When you think of sports in Japan, Sumo wrestling might be the first thing that comes to mind, and if you want to learn more about this unique sport, there's no better place to do so than at the Sumo Museum. There are thousands of artefacts in the museum, all relating to the history and culture of the sport. Inside, you will find the silk belts worn by fighters, sumo dolls, and multi-coloured woodblock prints.

84. Sip on the Best Espresso in Tokyo

If you can't function in the morning without a caffeine boost courtesy of a cup of coffee, you are in luck because although Japan might be more famous for its tea, the capital city has a thriving coffee culture. For our money, the very best place to sip on a strong and high quality espresso is at Bear Pond Espresso. The owner doesn't allow for anyone but himself to make the espresso, and he won't serve it after 2pm because he can't maintain a high enough quality. Now that is dedication to coffee.

85. Wash Your Money in the Zeniarai Benten Shrine

Kamakura is a small city that lies just an hour outside of Tokyo, so it's a great place to visit for the day if you want to escape the big city. When in Kamakura, one of our favourite things is to visit the Zeniarai Benten Shrine. This is an ancient shrine that was created in the early 12th century, and it is enduringly popular with visitors because it is said that if you wash your money in its on-site spring, your money will multiply in value.

86. Check out the Public Art of Taro Okamoto

For the local people on the streets of Tokyo, perhaps the most famous contemporary Japanese artist is Taro Okamoto. You can discover the works of the artist in the Taro Okamoto Museum of Art in the city, but it's more fun to walk around and spot his artworks that exist on the city streets. The painter originally created the "Myths of Tomorrow" painting in Mexico City, but it has since been transferred to the walls of the Shibuya metro station where it can now be enjoyed by commuters rushing to get to work.

87. Have the Best Burger of Your Life

You probably haven't trekked all the way to Tokyo to eat burgers, but let's face it, sometimes it is only a juicy burger that will do. And if you are hankering for a burger, you might just eat the best burger of your life at Brozer's Ginza. If you want to try the most impressive burger on the menu, be sure to order The Lot Burger, which includes a 100% beef patty in soft bread buns, crispy bacon, sweet pineapple, cheese, egg, a fried egg, and salad.

88. Pay Homage to Tokyo's Most Famous Dog

Hachiko is, without a doubt, the most famous dog in all of Japan. This dog was of the Akita breed, which is a breed from the mountains in the north of Japan. Every day, Hachiko used to meet his master at the same time outside Shibuya station, after his master finished his day of work. One day, his master died and never returned to the station, but the dog still returned to the same spot every day until he eventually died ten years later. Now, there is a statue erected outside of the station to commemorate this loving pooch.

89. Discover a World of Rice at Akomeya

Rice is the staple carbohydrate of Japanese cuisine, and you might not think that the world of rice is all that interesting, but you might just change your mind if you visit the Akomeya shop, which is totally dedicated to rice. There are so many rice items on display in the shop (6000 in fact!) that it can be somewhat overwhelming. You will be able to find rice bars of soap, rice wine, sweets made of rice, and lots more besides.

90. Find Something Special at the Tokyo International Art Fair

If you are an art lover, you can do one better than walking around the galleries of Tokyo, and plan your trip to coincide with the Tokyo International Art Fair, which is held every May. Over 150 artists from around the world are represented at the art fair, and if you are looking for something local, don't worry because there are works by plenty of Japanese artists on display. This could be just the place to find something really unique for your living room wall.

91. Indulge a Sweet Tooth With Taiyaki

While Japan is a country that is very well known for its food, most of the known dishes are savoury, but if you have a sweet tooth there is no need to worry because the country also has an assortment of sweet treats. Taiyaki has to be one of the cutest items of food you will ever eat. Taiyaki is essentially a fish shaped cake, usually made out of pancake batter, which is then filled with something like custard, red bean paste, chocolate, or sweet potato. These treats can be found all over Tokyo.

92. Catch a Show at the New National Theatre

If you are an arts lover, you will no doubt want to catch a show or two while you are in Tokyo, and we think that one of the best places to do so is at the New National Theatre. This theatre has three main stages, so it is able to stage a range of incredible productions at once. Check out the programme, and you are bound to be bowled over by the diversity of the productions. You'll find everything from Japanese opera performances to touring circus shows.

93. Relax in a Beautiful Tea Lounge

Of course, when in Tokyo, one of the things you have to do is drink plenty of relaxing tea. But if you don't want to head into a frantic tea shop in the middle of the city, you can instead sip on a hot cup of tea in a beautiful tea lounge called The Garden. It is located on the ground floor of the International House of Japan, which dates back to the 19th century, and the gardens there are still much as they were way back then. It's a beautiful place to take the weight off your shoulders for a moment.

94. Listen to Japanese Folk Music at Oiwake

Tokyo has a reputation for being a cutting edge city where you can experience the best of cosmopolitan 21st century living. While this is true, there are also places in the city where you can explore some older Japanese traditions. If you want to understand more about the folk music of the country, it's well worth spending an evening at Oiwake bar. They normally stage three folk performances a day, and you can order sashimi to accompany the performance, so it's well worth taking the time out for this experience.

95. Get Taken to the Tropics at the Aloha BBQ Beer Garden

If you fancy having a short break from Japanese culture, all you need to do is visit the Aloha BBQ Beer Garden where you will suddenly find yourself in tropical Hawaii. For the fairly decent price of 3000 yen (at least by Tokyo's standards), you can treat yourself to the Hawaiian BBQ set, which contains smoked beef, teriyaki chicken, spicy pork, and beers and pina coladas – yum!

96. Watch a Game at the Jingu Baseball Stadium

When you think of baseball, you might not immediately think of Japan. In fact, you definitely wouldn't think of Japan. But if you are a fan of the game and you fancy seeing some Japanese teams playing against each other, you can do so at the Jingu Baseball Stadium. This stadium opened in the 1920s and it can hold an astounding number of 38,000 spectators at any given time. Babe Ruth also played here so it's something of a pilgrimage site for baseball fanatics.

97. Become a Judo Master

Judo is a martial art created in Japan in the 19th century as a way of testing and improving both physical and mental ability. This martial art is now practised all over the world, but nowhere is it more popular than in the country of its birth, and if you want to learn some judo yourself, there are plenty of places where you can do so in Tokyo. The Kodokan in Tokyo is a place that caters to the needs of beginners to judo very well.

98. Be Wowed by the Tokyo Metropolitan Symphony Orchestra

If you are a classical music fan, you might be more tempted to visit somewhere like Prague or Budapest, but actually, Tokyo also has its own classical music culture, which is well worth exploring. The orchestra has been going strong since 1965, and if you get a chance to see them perform, you should grab at it with both hands. The orchestra regularly performs at the Tokyo Bunka Kaikan, Suntory Hall, and Tokyo Metropolitan Theatre.

99. Sip on Sake at Kuri

Sake is the national drink of Japan, a type of rice wine that is made by fermenting rice that has been polished. Of course, there is no shortage of opportunities to sip on sake while you're in Tokyo, but perhaps the best sake bar of them all in Japan's capital city is Kuri. Over 100 varieties of sake are stocked behind the bar at any given time, and they also change their sake menu seasonally, so each week there is something new to try.

100. Party Until Dawn at ageHA

Want to party until the early hours of the morning and dance with Tokyo locals on the dancefloor? Then you need to hit the clubs, and specifically, ageHA. If you are serious about dance music, this is the place to party because the club has previously hosted world renowned DJs such as Tiesto and Paul Van Dyck. Something we really love about the space is that it also has an outdoor terrace and pool, which goes down a storm in the summer months.

101. Eat a Decadent Meal at Kohaku

It is no secret that a trip to Tokyo can be difficult for the budget, but there are times when you just have to throw caution to the wind and splurge on something that you really want. If you love great food and stunning restaurants, you need to reserve a table at Kohaku, which has two Michelin stars, and serves up contemporary Japanese cuisine. Order the tasting menu, and you can try a bit of everything, from sea urchin with white sesame tofu to green tea mousse with brandy sorbet.

Before You Go…

Thanks for reading **101 Coolest things to Do in Tokyo**. We hope that it makes your trip a memorable one!

If you enjoyed this book, we'd really appreciate it if you could leave a review on our Amazon page – thanks a million!

Keep your eyes peeled on www.101coolestthings.com, and have a great trip!

Team 101 Coolest Things

Printed in Great Britain
by Amazon